The Bachelors' Club

-

Jack's Curated Business Idea

-

Jack Lookman

The Bachelors' Club

Jack's Curated Business Idea

Copyright © 2024 Jack Lookman Limited

A. ACKNOWLEDGEMENT

I'm continuously grateful to my Creator and Sustainer, for known and unknown favours, blessings and protection.

I appreciate my parents, for being my vehicle of success.

I was fortified with spiritual and academic knowledge and practices; as well as great life skills.

Contributions of John Tosin Adekunle are much appreciated.

I appreciate my siblings, who've supported me directly and indirectly.

My beautiful Tolu Mayowa Tobi you are very much appreciated.

I appreciate all my Teachers, both formal and informal - Thank you very much.

To all those who've added value to me in one way or the other, I say, thank you.

To my Creator and Sustainer: Alhamdu lillahi rabbi alAAalameena.

B. DEDICATION

This piece of work is dedicated to all my family members.

My Late Dad

My Mum

My Siblings

My Children

Ire awawa ri o. (May you find the blessings that you desire)

Ire aje'n jetan (May our Creator and Sustainer grant us everlasting blessings)

May Allah grant us goodness in this world and the hereafter and protect us from the torment of hell fire. Ameen.

C. CONTENT

D. Preamble

Is there sometimes opportunity in adversity?
And prosperity in opportunity?

If you think outside the box...
Could you enjoy a monopoly?
And monetise uncontrollably?

If you explore your creativity...
And articulate it into opportunity...
And give value to your audience...

Could you leave a worthwhile legacy?
And benefit generations unborn?

If there's an enabling environment...
One that brings out the best in you...
Giving you an opportunity to thrive....

Could it benefit all of us?

If we live our lives...
Doing our very best...
Empowering and inspiring...

Could we ever be losers?

This is my little contribution...

A give back to humanity...

So that when I'm long gone...

It could still benefit some.

For those watching on YouTube, at 'Curated Business Ideas' the video is timestamped for ease of reference.

Hello, greetings to one and all. Welcome to <u>Jack's Curated Business Ideas</u>. Today's topic is

The Bachelors' Club.

Some marriages fail, because expectations are not fully managed. Many fail due to lack of preparedness. Meanwhile, others fail due to the wrong mindset, and some, due to incompatibility.

With this business model, we intend to proactively groom bachelors for marriage.

It will be a user-led online activity where different aspects of marriage will be explored; professionals will facilitate the process and experienced husbands will be involved. Also, newly-weds and potential husbands will be involved.

Rather than impose what is right or wrong on the client, the idea is to explore rhetorical questions and then allow the potential husbands make individual conclusions.

1. Value Proposition

We shall be proactively helping adult males make informed decisions on marriage by leveraging the internet.

2. Process

You can create your curriculum, do marketing, arrange meetings, send reminders to attendees and semi-automate processes.

Also, you can have your rules and regulations, sort out legalities, articulate discussion points, moderate meetings, signpost your audience to more content and mentors, give homework to your attendees and have a registration process in place.

3. Number of Participants

Each session can have up to five to ten clients depending on your judgment call. This could be more manageable and more effective, enabling a personal touch. Depending on the topic at hand and logistics, a professional, experienced husband or recent husband may be in attendance, individually or collectively.

4. Curriculum

This shall include the full range, from pre-marriage, marriage, to post-marriage. It shall also include parenting, spirituality, case studies, sexual issues, in-laws, sickness, death, etc.

5. Digital Content

There shall be complementary digital content, which shall be updated as necessary. This could be on different platforms, such as social media, blogs, membership sites, podcasts etc.

6. Marketing Considerations

You may want to consider:

• Digital marketing
• Social media marketing
• Influencer marketing
• Testimonials
• Search Engine Optimisation (SEO)
• Content marketing
• Word of mouth

- Print marketing
- Radio marketing
- Digital marketer
- DIY marketing - *do it yourself.*
- Content marketing website
- Blog
- And marketing, generally.
- WhatsApp marketing
- Sales funnel
- Collaborations
- Front links, back links and internal links

7. Benefits

These include:

- Networking
- Opportunities
- Useful knowledge dissemination
- Added societal value
- Wealth creation
- Job creation
- Marital round pegs to round holes
- Monetisation
- Education
- Reduced divorce rate
- More productive society
- Minimised conflicts
- Etc

8. Unique Selling Proposition

The business model is a proactive way of empowering bachelors to learn and make informed decisions on marriage by leveraging the internet.

9. Costing Thoughts

These include: digital devices, human resources, <u>Profit Sharing Formula App</u>, communication network, time, marketing, profit margin, number of clients, competition, discounts, logistics, etc.

10. Pricing Considerations

These include: profit margin, cost of delivery, affordability of customers, volume of clients, demand and supply, complimentary products and services, sales funnel, <u>Profit Sharing Formula App</u> , competition in the market place, operational costs, capital cost, etc.

11. Frequency of the Meetings

The time and frequency of meetings shall be agreed between stakeholders and the clients.

It could be weekly, fortnightly, monthly etc.

Depending on the agreement, the duration of each session could be an hour, 30 minutes or 45 minutes, etc.

You will also need to agree on the time of the day that the sessions will take place; it could be in the morning, afternoon or evening.

You also need to decide on the day or days of the week. These could be during the week day (in the evenings), or anytime during weekends, as agreed.

You should consider global time differences if your clients are located in different countries or time zones.

12. What problem are you solving?

You will help reduce the rate of divorces and help educate men on intricacies of marriage. You shall add value to society, to marriages, to the marriage institution, and reduce marital conflict.

13. Profit Sharing Formula

A profit-sharing formula app could be used for effective, fair and just profit sharing among business stakeholders. The team will share profits based on agreed criteria and the profit-sharing formula app tracks this effectively.

14. Funding

The business model is not expected to be costly; the stakeholders could finance the business or get outsiders to finance it. The profit-sharing formula app could be used in effecting fair sharing of profits. Funding could be got through crowdfunding, stakeholder funding, investors, bank loan, or loan from family and friends, etc.

15. Requirements for Club Membership

There shall be an application process. Applicants have to fit into your criteria. They need to have a digital device, and internet access. They also need to be proactive, make payment and be committed.

16. Business Requirements

These include digital devices, administration, internet connection, human resources, zoom or other communication platforms, membership site, social media platforms, marketers and advertisers, information technology leads. You also need to invest in research and development; as well as Training & Development.

17. Monetisation

- You could leverage multiple platforms such as social media, membership sites, books (via amazon or alternatives), blog, podcast, etc.
- There shall be payments for sessions, for example 1 to 1's, or 1 to many.
- You could do affiliate marketing on your platforms.
- You could do public speaking
- You could include paid adverts on your platforms
- You could leverage collaborations
- You could offer consultancy to individuals and organisations.

18. Suggested payment plans

Payments could be made quarterly, biannually or annually.
You could offer discounts, based on different factors, such as the longevity of your association, receptiveness of the client, the amount of purchases made, introduction of other clients, etc.

19. Payment Gateways

This could be through:

- Stripe
- PayPal
- Pay and Earn
- Flutter wave
- Etc

20. Refund Policy

Research and include this in your contract. This helps with expectation management and reduction or avoidance of conflict. There are also templates online; pick, choose and edit as necessary.

21. Target Demographics

These could include undergraduates, fresh graduates, graduates, Muslims, Christians, other religious groups, adults, youths, Nigerians, Yoruba, Hausas, Igbos, diasporas, other ethnicities, etc.

It could also include divorcees, widowers, older men, those who share common values, community groups, or it could be a combination of the above.

22. Team.

These could include marriage counsellor, experienced husband, a recent husband, religious clerics, content creator, experienced wife, a recent wife, widow, widower, divorcees, entrepreneur, marketer, etc.

There could be duplication of roles by individuals, and some of those mentioned above will be Ad hoc team members.

They will also be anonymous as necessary. They shall be invited to sessions as necessary.

23. Platform

- This shall be online, through:
- Zoom
- Google Meet
- Social Media
- WhatsApp

• Or suitable others

24. Disclaimer

This is just a business idea and not and an end in itself. You need to perfect it to suit your business objectives.

25. Value Chain

These include content creation, marketing, knowledge dissemination, blogging, book authoring, content marketing, brainstorming, etc.

26. Legalities

You need to put legalities in place. In addition to the refund policy, you need to include terms and conditions, disclaimers, legal agreements or contracts, with all related parties. These include with clients, stakeholders and any other related third parties.

27. What is your product or service?

In simple understandable language, it is an organised set of online sessions, where adult men are counselled and educated on marriage and its pros and cons so that they can make informed decision before embarking on the journey of marriage.

28. Can this business be scaled?

I think it can. You could replicate the business model to different niches. For example, the same model can be replicated for spinsters, Muslims, Christians, other religious groups, and other demographics. It could be for different age demographics, cultures, ethnicities, countries and diasporas.

You could also have a franchise.

29. Income Streams

These could include books, online content, premium products and services, as well as 1 to 1 sessions. As well as membership sites, blogs, affiliate marketing, podcast, adverts on your platforms, social media channels, mentoring, dating websites, gift service, grooming of bachelors, grooming of spinsters, optimal job search services, and income optimisation opportunities.

After all, if you are going to be a husband, you need to have a good income to support the family.

As a business, you could offer this as a service, collaborate with others, or include Affiliate Marketing links on your platforms. You could also delve into content and related services on parental skills, etc.

30. Perks

As perks to your clients, you could offer discounts on products and services; you could make them affiliate marketers of your products and services and give them generous commissions.

For those who perform exceptionally; you could offer them additional perks such as free complementary products and services, or give additional discounts, or you could collaborate with them.

31. Exit strategy for Clients

They could terminate the engagement at any point and they could give notice or not, depending on the contract they signed. They may get a refund, if your policy permits. Also, they could assign their unused product and services to relevant others or come to an agreement with you on this.

32. Exit Strategy for Stakeholders

The <u>profit-sharing formula app</u> probably addresses this. Alternatively, the related legal documents could address it.

All documents or agreements could be amended as necessary.

If the agreement does not effectively address the issue, there shall be mutual and fair agreement on the resolution. Or you might involve a conflict resolution agent to mediate.

The agreement could then be updated accordingly, to avoid a repeat scenario.

33. Conclusion

This content is an attempt at marrying creativity, technology, entrepreneurship, social cohesion, education, etc.
It's one of those out of the box thoughts.
In as much as it may be imperfect, it's hoped that you could perfect it to meet your needs.
It's hoped that you got some value, and that it could benefit yourself, your network, society and humanity.
Thank you very much for your time.

God bless you.

34. Disclaimer

We are also affiliate marketers. We promote products and services of ourselves and third parties and get monetised at no additional cost to you.

The curated business ideas on these and our other platforms are born out of creativity, experience, and exposure. You are expected to modify them to suit your needs.

Inasmuch as they are great ideas, they don't guarantee financial success.

There are many determining factors for success to be achieved. You are expected to carry out due diligence before embarking on any entrepreneurial pursuits.

35. Mission

Our mission at Jack Lookman Limited is to empower and Inspire Generations by leveraging the internet.

36. Did you get value?

We hope that you got some value from this content, learnt 1 or 2 things, and that it stimulated your thoughts; if so, please consider sharing with others as well as sharing your comments.

If you wish to discuss this further or to embark on any of Jack's Curated Business Ideas, please, search for 'Business Collaboration With Jack Lookman' online, or visit Jack's Empowerment.

Also, you could send a short email to info@jacklookmanlimited.com and we shall respond.

You could 'Book A Chat With Jack Lookman' at jacksempowerment.com

You could get more of such content, on our different platforms on social media. You could find us on Youtube, Facebook, TikTok, LinkedIn, etc. Just do a search for Jack Lookman or search for curated business idea or Curated Business Ideas.

You could also access content on our websites:
Jack's Empowerment which is a membership site.
Curated Business Ideas - a blog
Jaaloo Puzzles - jaaloopuzzles.com - jaaloo.com
Jack Lookman Limited - jacklookmanlimited.com
Life Lessons For Teenagers - lifelessonsforteenagers.com

We've also written many books. Please search for Jack Lookman's books on the internet, or visit jacklookmanlimited.com

- You could also join Jack Lookman's community on Facebook.
- We create content
- We mentor
- We do affiliate marketing
- We do business collaborations
- And app development collaborations

- We've authored and published several books on
  - curated business ideas
  - mindset
  - poetry
  - Jaaloo Puzzles

- Etc

- If you are interested in playing an arithmetic number game called Jaaloo Puzzles, it's a very good brain exercise for children, adults, youths and the elderly. It helps with accuracy skills, mental alertness, competition skills, arithmetic and logic skills. You could find it at jaaloo.com and jaaloopuzzles.com

- Are you interested in Business Collaboration With Jack Lookman ?
- Or in Jack's Mentoring 101 ?
- If yes, search for it or them at jacksempowerment.com

37. Useful compliments

1. Jack's Empowerment - membership site - jacksempowerment.com
2. Jaaloo Puzzles - blog - jaaloopuzzles.com
3. Curated Business Ideas - blog - curatedbusinessideas.com
4. Jack Lookman Limited - blog - jacklookmanlimited.com
5. Youtube channel: Curated Business Ideas
6. Youtube channel: Jaaloo Puzzles
7. Youtube channel: Life Lessons For Teenagers
8. Facebook: Jack Lookman
9. Facebook: Curated Business Ideas
10. Facebook: Jaaloo Puzzles
11. Facebook: Life Lessons For Teenagers
12. Jack Lookman's Books

13. Business Collaboration With Jack Lookman - jacksempowerment.com
14. Jack's Mentoring 101 - jacksempowerment.com
15. Youtube video: Empowering The Less Educated
16. Facebook video: Empowering The Less Educated
17. Life Lessons For Teenagers : lifelessonsforteenagers.com
18. Book A Chat With Jack Lookman : jacksempowerment.com

38. Some Useful Links:

Facebook Community: Jack Lookman

Youtube channel: Curated Business Ideas

Facebook group: Curated Business Ideas

Jack Lookman's Books

Jack Lookman Websites

39. Useful hashtags

1. #jackscuratedbusinessidea
2. #jackscuratedbusinessideas
3. #JaalooPuzzles
4. #CuratedBusinessIdeas
5. #JackLookmanLimited
6. #ireo
7. #Irekabiti
8. #JackLookman

9. #empoweringandinspiringgenerations
10. #EmpowermentandInspiration

40. Books by Jack Lookman

Visit:

- jacklookmanlimited.com
- Internet search? Jack Lookman
- Or Jack Lookman's Books

41. Some resources by Jack Lookman

- Jack's Empowerment - jacksempowerment.com
- Jaaloo Puzzles - jaaloopuzzles.com
- Jaaloo Puzzles - jaaloo.com
- Curated Business Ideas curatedbusinessideas.com
- Life Lessons For Teenagers : lifelessonsforteenagers.com
- Youtube channel: Curated Business Ideas
- Youtube channel: Life Lessons For Teenagers
- Facebook: Jack Lookman
- Facebook group: Curated Business Ideas
- Facebook group: Menteero
- Facebook group: Jaaloo Puzzles
- Facebook group: Life Lessons For Teenagers
- Etc.

42. Will you like to collaborate?

Does the Jack Lookman brand resonate with you? Will you like to collaborate? If yes, please send an email to: info@jacklookmanlimited.com

Use an appropriate subject heading and narrative.

43. Will you like to be mentored by Jack Lookman?

If yes, please send an email to: info@jacklookmanlimited.com

Use an appropriate subject heading and narrative.

You could also check our websites:

- Jack's Empowerment: - jacksempowerment.com
- Jaaloo Puzzles - jaaloo.com
- Jack's Mentoring 101: jacksempowerment.com
- Business Collaboration With Jack Lookman - jacksempowerment.com
- Jaaloo Puzzles - jaaloopuzzles.com
- Curated Business Ideas - curatedbusinessideas.com
- Jack Lookman Limited - jacklookmanlimited.com
- Life Lessons For Teenagers - lifelessonsforteenagers.com

44. Social media:

Some of our platforms are:

Facebook - Jack Lookman - Facebook profile - https://www.facebook.com/jack.lookman.3

Facebook group: Curated Business Ideas

Youtube channel: Curated Business Ideas

TikTok: jacklookman4

LinkedIn: Olayinka Carew aka Jack Lookman

45. Our books could be found at:

Amazon: - amazon.co.uk - search for Jack Lookman

Find a comprehensive list at jacklookmanlimited.com

Or check other reputable book shops.

46. OTHER PUBLICATIONS BY JACK LOOKMAN LIMITED

1. *Despair, Submission, Faith and Hope – Volume 1*

2. *Despair, Submission, Faith and Hope – Volume 2*

3. *Monetising Digital Book Reviews*

4. *E-Commerce For Traditional African Attires*

5. *Basic Management And Fundraising Tip For Community Groups*

6. *Monetising A Digital Library*

7. *Ajo, The App And Opportunities*

8. *Empowering Orphans, Widows and Widowers*

9. *Submission, Gratitude, Faith and Hope*

10. *Oro Ishiti- Indelible Yoruba Words - Adebanji Osanyingbemi*

11. *Eid Monetisation by Leveraging Technology*

12. *What are your thoughts? What is your mindset? - Volume 1*

47. About Jack Lookman

Olayinka Carew, aka Jack Lookman is the 1st of 5 Children.
He has 3 children, and an elderly mum. He is resident in the
United Kingdom and is of Nigerian origin.

He studied at King's College, Lagos and University of Lagos.
He has varied life and work experiences.
He has been involved in voluntary and paid jobs.

He is dedicating the rest of his life to empowering and inspiring generations.

This is one of his legacy projects.

Though he has health challenges, he does not let that impede his mission and vision.

Even though he studied Engineering in University; his calling is so many miles away from that. He is currently an Entrepreneur, Content Creator, Affiliate Marketer, Volunteer, Business Collaborator and Mentor.

He is the Director and Owner of Jack Lookman Limited, a registered business in the United Kingdom; and their aim is to empower and inspire generations by leveraging the internet.

This is Jack Lookman signing off. Ire o (I wish you blessings)

Ire kabiti (I wish you loads of blessings).